Love or Nothing

by the same author

TERRY STREET
THE HAPPIER LIFE
A CHOICE OF BYRON'S VERSE (*editor*)

Love or Nothing

DOUGLAS DUNN

FABER & FABER
3 Queen Square, London

First published in 1974
by Faber and Faber Limited
3 Queen Square London WC1
Printed in Great Britain by
Latimer Trend & Company Ltd Plymouth

ISBN 0 571 10614 5

Contents

Little Rich Rhapsody

For he has spent the summer in hotels
Of eight resorts. His miniature cocotte,
That handful of the mouthfuls, pleased him well.
Expensive, though; within a month he'd bought
More cunning clothes for her than used to pack
Mother's wardrobe, that sly adulteress
Who, when she died, left nothing but those clothes
In the Paris flat, the London flat, the villas,
Clothes on their wooden hangers, hanging slack
Just as she lived, he lives. Ah, happiness
Of hired cars and views of France, all those
Who stop at nothing and who thrill us
With rapid spendings, dissolutions through
Such finery of clothes of white and blue!

The House Next Door

Old dears gardening in fur coats
And 'Hush Puppies', though it's a mild July,
Once met Freddie Lonsdale at John o' Groats.
Their keyboard's Chopin and their humour's wry.
    There's no one I'd rather be called 'famous' by.
    They have an antique goldfish, a cat called Sly.

They live in my unpublished play
For two sad characters. Their Chippendale
Haunts England's salesrooms, their silver tray
That brought Victoria's breakfast and her mail.
    I visit their house—its coffee aroma,
    The cat out cold in its afternoon coma!

I watch them watching for the post,
Wondering who writes. In *my* play, no one writes,
They are alone, together, and have lost
Our century by being old. Their nights
    Are spent rehearsing through Irving Berlin;
    The gardens turn to stage-sets when they begin.

My best times with them are 'Chopin
Mornings'. They smile vainly at my small applause—
No one plays the Pole as badly as they can—
And Sly stands up, and purrs, stretching his claws,
    Playing his cat's piano on the cushions,
    And called by pianist sisters, Perfect Nuisance.

There garage is pronounced gar*age*,
Strawberries never known as strawbs, but *fraises*,
And cheddar is called cheese, the rest *fromage*,
And all life is a lonely Polonaise.
    Why do I love them, that milieu not mine,
    The youngest, laughingly, 'last of the line'?

No answers. They have given me
Too much for answering. I am their pet,
Like Sly. They have defied me, cutting free
From my invention. 'Let us live. Forget
    You made us up for money. We'll give you tea,
And you shall drive our ancient crock down to the sea.'

Winter Graveyard

Moss-obelisk and moss-gloved curves
Of uncherishable headstones
Rise from the dead place at the time of death.
A swarm of fissured angels sweeps over
Unremarkable civilians,
Magnates of no inheritance;
In depths of briar and ivy
Their utterly negative remains—
Dried convolvulus,
A bush of nerves sprouted
From lost anatomies.

Survivors of scattered families
Can't get at inscriptions.
When did Frederick die? Or Emily?
They need to know, relatives
Underfoot impart a sad feeling
Worth expeditions
Sometimes beaten back by the strength
Of wild entanglements
Pensioners declare is neglect, unprincipled
Spite of generation for generation,
And imply their own regret.

How can they bear to know they are
Now similarly doomed
In a city not even a metropolis,
And their cross a broken ornament?
Even that era of grand proprieties,
Domain of the picture-hook and claw-footed table,

Its offering servants,
Is sunk and forgotten,
Submerged under midget Gothic;
Fast sycamores grow
Upright out of Victorian creeper.

This is the door to Victoria's heaven.
To sink one's face in a cushion
And share as if from an alms box
Love preserved in Death,
Its hundred-thousand sentiments—
The man who came from the house
With the dancers to talk of the summer,
A soldier who told Edwardian merchants
Of a minor campaign in Assam.
They dance now to secret ragtime
In red-plush joints.

Once they were blue citizenry
At the end of streets, in horse-traffic.
If I shut my eyes
They are still there, in the same stillness;
The same harmonious dusk
Of a generation whose male children—
Young in 1914—
Are not buried here
But died abroad defending an Empire's
Affectionate stability
And an industry of lies.

Rank everlastingness
Mud-buttered;
Money is this,
One old penny at the edge of a grave,
Shrill starlings over

Columns and sarcophagi, as many as
The corners hiding God
Here, in his formal dump.
Rubbish of names under vomit of moss;
Inscriptions incised
In thin velvet

Rinse their loving vocabularies
In the light of dreams.
And I am momentarily disabled
By the thought that this is real-pink sky
Behind the black upreaching trees,
Aspirations of beauty and love
Disregarding corroded vulgarity
And farcical monuments
To sanctities not worth the enshrinement
That outlast memory and money.
And a white bird leaves a bare tree.

Winter Orchard

Five days of fog over snow,
Thinning, thickening, thinning
Before dark,
Its last substantial grit,
A breath with industry on it.

Blank miseries
Of the average dead;
Miscellaneous, unspectacular visitation;
Spiritual dregs
Out of the gutters of what-drab-Heaven,

The City of what-suburbanly-managerial-God?
Cold torpor of questions,
Revenge of the unfructified,
Yesterday,
The ash that looks like air.

Emerging, sailing,
Unrescuable grey-drenched browns
Of unpruned apple trees,
Their crush of twigs;
Threat of unleafed forks.

An apple is still stuck there,
Almost yellow in this light.
One survivor of harvest;
Unreachable,
It flourished but came to nothing.

Best efforts are negative,
Seriously beautiful, like art.
Clear light speaks valediction;
Sparse branches
In an orchard of goodbyes,

So many lines that spume or trail off
Beyond limits, their own reaches.
The sky is a net of black nerves,
Continued dream-lines of trees.
Fog's majesty,

Sheer strength of numbers, departs;
Swish of moth-eaten cloaks,
Coarse garments——
Generation upon labouring generation
Of conscripts and grocers' assistants,

Millhands, the unnamed courtiers
Of long-dead industrial magnates.
Their souls shine
On wet slates in summer, sliced turn
Of an autumn furrow, a now-sacred pippin,

As the snow melts like white grease
And soot-spotted stalactites vanish
In their own directions
To destinations that are sounds and wetness;
A soft, cold world
That grows dark when fog clears,
The ground that receives the apple.

In the Small Hotel

There they must live forever, under soft lights,
The cheated at their favourite separate tables,
Inactive thirds of tender adulteries.

They stare into a light that is always evening,
Their eyes divided, as if distracted by
The ghost of something only one eye sees

Sleep-walking in plastic darkness
Around the night-clubs. They sit like chessmen
At their white round squares, waiting to be moved.

No one makes conversation. A hand
May absently arrange roses in a vase
Or wave away the leering gypsy fiddler.

Chefs please no one there and the waiters stamp
Untipped among customers too vague and lost
To ever think of coming back to commerce.

People we did not want or could not keep;
Someone did this to them, over and over
Wanting their unhappiness until it happened.

Over the dewy grass with a small suitcase
Love comes trotting and stops to hold on a shoe.
To go away with *her*! To drive the limousine

With contraceptives in the glove compartment
Beside the chocolates and packaged orchid
And find that new Arcadia replacing Hollywood!

Remote and amatory, that style of life
In which no one offends or intrudes.
They might as well live in their wardrobes.

The Global Fidget

Miss E., so kind and clean, once Mrs. S.,
But now 'reverted back', as Miss E. says,
Is tidy at the picnic, holding wine.
She talks about her 'loves', such anodyne
Remembrances, and can't help being trite.
But we excuse her faith—Miss E. is tight.

Dear Edith Ermine, we once thought you brave.
That horseback expedition with a slave
You'd freed in Berbera inspired us through
Our teens. I had such high regard for you
In all my girlhood, and your postcards meant
Such satisfaction and such discontent,

Still growing up straight-laced and bored
With school, dull friends, and the routinely-scored
And endless tennis. My friends were *not* dull;
By being gone, you made me act the fool,
Wanting to be with you, alive and far
Strolling that market place at Kandahar,

And snapped with white-socked officers, and wooed
By potentates. Today the word is 'screwed',
But you, prim mother's sister, my dear aunt,
Are broke and loveless, quite ignored, and can't,
For all your tales, disguise the fact that travel
Is nothing to experience, a drivel

Of distance and an obstacle of seas
To cross and reach your trivial ecstacies.

And now, half cut, or 'tipsy' as you say,
You woo my daughter with the midnight day
Of Lapland, followed by the Karroo heat,
Adventures in the Andamans. Dead beat

Of expeditionary life, you roved,
I know. I'd love you for it, if you'd proved
Your own affections, given proof, just once,
Of selflessness, and love. And now the chance
Is that my daughter will grow up like me,
Wanting your sort of past, the rich and free

Lady traveller of the China Seas,
Sister to warlords, nurse of missionaries.
Long-skirted, overland Herodotus,
Dear Edith, aunt, what will become of us?
You have successes, failures, like the rest,
And I am static. Your way of life is best?

Broke and put up by disenchanted friends
Bored with your reminiscence of the ends
Of geography, you look forward to *us*,
Your complicated nieces, and our fuss
Of children, husbands, thinking that you please,
Opening the atlas of your memories.

Realisms

(To Derek Mahon)

Poetry in a flap,
Its paper efficiencies
Thoth with an accent.

Details shrug me off,
Rain from a wet coat;
I am shoulders.

You have the same concern;
The real stuff hurts, efforts
To write it down confuse,

Or soothe too much, having
Too many ideas to start with,
Too many words.

Whittling down
An algebra of 'sympathies'
Through brilliant sums

To a sudden Nothing,
We find a glimpse of housing estates,
A duster on a window

Waving to a street
Its goodbyes to the spirit
Of domestic energies.

At the moist limits
Of Zero, where worlds turn
Vegetable or wiry

And politics dissolve,
Gunfire is silent.
Its echo reached us here,

Far down in France, the thud
That hits the citizens who die
For random's cause—

The cause of being them,
Of being there, blown to pieces
As they drink their tea.

I am against most revolutions,
All conformities. You must demur.
At least, raise your eyebrows.

Nothing helps.
Our fatuous surrender
To the language deals

No impertinence or blow.
We puff our alphabets
Back to the oratorical soup

Of Ireland, Scotland,
To a thousand stabs in the back,
The inhabitants of opposition.

Our cities of shipyards,
Belfast, Glasgow, fervent closures
Of protestantism dispensed with—

We never escape them,
Returning to stale dreams,
Old possibilities, dismissed

In the eyes of generators
Of what we kicked from our heels,
And friends who stayed

To admonish our absences.
Streets, an altered skyline,
The half-remembered face

Of an early girl-friend
We might almost have married
Under the trees of the playground—

And the dream comes back,
Again and again, far away
At the ends of roads,

The existential clarity
Of love and nothing, the peace
Poets in patched trousers deserve.

Renfrewshire Traveller

Home rain, an aerial night-Clyde,
Spray of recollection
And my only appropriate welcome.

Have I come back?
It was dark
Through Kilmarnock,

Johnny Walker blinked
Imperfectly; history
Is whisky, *lacrimae rerum.*

Have I come back?
I am Scots, a tartan tin box
Of shortbread in a delicatessen of cheddars

And southern specialties.
I am full of poison.
Each crumb of me is a death,

Someone you never see again
After funerals in the rain.
Men who return wearing black ties,

Men who return having looked for work—
Hear them, their Glasgow accents
In the night of high-rise

Skyward tenements, railway platforms,
The accents of rain and arguments.
What have I come to?

Not this. Not this
Slow afright over rails,
This ache in a buffet of empty beer-cans.

This wiping of windows to see a city
Rise from its brilliant lack,
Its fixtures in transparent butter.

Not this visitor
To a place of relatives,
A place of names.

Unlucky Mariners

Clapped out, with long necks
And thin bodies pivoting
On paunches,
They sit like unstrung banjos
Waiting their names to be called.

I dream of rusting hulks
In the Indies,
Jammed among the mangrove
Where sea stops inch by inch,
Water, snakes and vegetable are one.

'John Rigg, you spilled your rum
From Stornoway to the dreary Plate.
I saw you wench Malacca
Under the palms;
You changed your ladies with the tide.'

Dance of the shingle resort,
Fore-shore trash
And harbour-masters counting
Prosperity by tonnage—
Here are the makers of music,

The numbers missed by arithmetic,
Unshipped and down on their luck
As they have been down on their luck
In disgusting jails
Near all the harbours.

'MacBryde, you shipped out of Glasgow
In '32, and you're back
With five German duckings
And thoughts of as many bastards
As you've had slit-skirted slope-eyed whores.'

Once, on a raft on a lagoon
Of Renfrewshire's Clyde,
An old man waved from his freighter;
He had nothing to do but wave to me,
And I thought, 'I'll go to sea.'

I dream of rusting hulks
And undersea
The leaky tubs that God's torpedo
Plugged; in South Pacific huts
The lucky mariners, copra kings

With four wives and the respect
Of The Islands,
Playing much-repaired concertinas
Long into the night,
To the tropical stars.

And I look at this lot,
Calling out their names
From *The Ledger of Missing Seafarers*,
So seldom called
They think I call their fathers.

Their grey skins are radiant mist,
Their eyes deep pools
In which the monsters sleep—
From nautical boyhoods
To skeletal service on The Ghost Ship.

'Falkenberg, you've a lot
To answer for. Your slummy crew
Picked off the bobbing wrecks
Might answer to your bells
But you're shipless now.'

Wrecks of many seas,
Here by the silent shipyards
Of the shore, ghosts of nuts and bolts
Toast your epiphanies
In the transparent grave of the fish!

Ocean

Beneath continuous seas, the wrecks
Of sunken thalassocracies;
Lost submarines, still gliding
To their secret fathoms—magnificence
And magnitude of hulks.

Airless battleships have fallen
With shoals of nibbling fish
Into the oceanic mouths
Of seven shapes—more bullion there
Than fills the teeth of galaxies.

Port Logan and a Vision of Live Maps

Cartographical morass
And the dissolve of speculation;
Strabo in the poop
Studying the periplum . . .

Infinity of routes where steel wanders,
Clydeside machinery . . .
And here is my gift from the sea,
A bobbing grapefruit that comes in on a wave.

The Scar

In the days of my scar
    Go-chaired among the uniforms
Of the Home Fleet
    A boy

What was first in my mind
    The dark rafts of our submarines
Strung at anchor
    The sun

Shone on the Firth, blinding
    One silhouetted guard, walking
Loch houses stiff
    With views

Our still flotillas flagged
    Our war-returned, ditched battleboats
Heaved on their chains
    At peace

And I had to fall in
    Down to the jellyfish and leech
Dining upon
    Rough stone

Reducing it to red
    To harm a child, war does attract
The nurse, the stitch
    Nothing

Good to have fallen then
    I am my friends, the casualties
One accident
    One scar

Sunday

Fat women in blue overalls
Washed locomotives in the railway yards
    I saw how naked their hands were
    One hour before my mother took
    Flowers to her dead

Our hands against the railings
And women workers with their pails and suds
    White soap foam on the shining green
    The space between rust-railings!
    Our hands, so naked

Killed forty years before my birth
Grandfather's brother's death I liked, more sad
    In a quarry, the story went
    Most words are good as useless, blah
    Chasing a rabbit

But the same hands, the same flowers
A loveable indifference

White Fields

An aeroplane, its red and green night-lights
Spotting its distant noise in the darkness;
'Jack Frost', you say, pointing to white fields
Sparkling. My eyes accept the dark, the fields
Extend, spreading and drifting, fences rising
Before the black hedge that zips beside the road
I'm told I must never try to cross without you.
'What time is it?'—'The middle of the night!
You've had a dream, I heard you shout.'
It woke me and I cried aloud, until
My mother came and showed me the farm
Wasn't burning, the school still had its roof,
There was no one hidden in the little fir trees.
'Only an aeroplane!' As if you meant by that
That there in 1948 in Renfrewshire
We were safe from fear, and the white eyes
Of dead Jews were just photographs
In a terrible past, a neighbour's magazine.
'Only an aeroplane!' Unsleeping factories,
All night you busied overhead, and flames
Flushed out my cities made of shoe-boxes
And dominoes, my native village of shaws.
So innocent machine! I had a toy like you
That I made buzz and drone like Leaper's bees,
From which I dropped the A-bomb on John's pram,
Crumpling the hand-embroidered sheets.
  Our breath melted ice on the window-pane.
Fields drizzled on the glass, opening strips
Of short-lived clarity, and fingernails of ice
Slid to the sill. 'No harm will come to us.'

I slept. Till now I've slept, dreaming of mice
Burrowing under the crusted tufts of snow
That heaviest fall had left us with,
Our planet flooded into continents
Of stray, white islands, a sea too cold to swim.
Till now I've slept, and waking, I reject
Your generation, an old copy of *Everybody's*
Thrown out with *Film Fun* and the tea leaves,
Bulldozed by a conscript from our village
Into a pit dug by forced labour.
So easily is love shed, I hardly feel it.
   White fields, your angled frost filed sharply
Bright over undisturbed grasses, do not soothe
As similes of innocence or idle deaths
That must happen anyway, an unmoral blankness;
Be unforgiving stillness, natural, what is:
Crimes uttered in landscape, smoke-darkened snow.
   Trains in my distance altered. Cattle trucks
Seemed to chug through Georgetown, a station
Where a fat man in a black uniform kept hens
On the platform. The waggons sprouted arms
And dropped dung, and no one sang
'Ten Green Bottles' or 'The Sash.' Offensive outings.

Six years old! And I lived through the worst of it!

The Competition

When I was ten, going to Hamilton
On the Leyland bus named for Eddlewood,
A boy with an aeroplane just like mine
Zoomed at his war games in the seat in front.
I'd never seen such a school uniform—
As brown as the manure in Cousar's coup
Where someone's city cousin had jumped in
Having been told it was 'just sand'—
One of Glasgow's best fee-paying places,
Brown as barrowloads from the blue-bottled byre.
I couldn't help it; I had to talk to him
And tell him I, too, had a Hurricane.
His mother pulled him to her, he sat sullen,
As if I'd spoiled his game. I spoke again,
And he called me a poor boy, who should shut up.
I'd never thought of it like that.
The summer tenements were so dry I cried.
My grandfather wouldn't give *him* sixpence;
He'd never have a grudge as lovely as mine.

Years later, running in a race, barefooted
As I'd trained my spikes to ruin, convinced
My best competitor was him, I ran into
The worst weathers of pain, determined to win,
But on the last lap, inches from the tape, was beaten
By someone from Shotts Miners' Welfare Harriers Club.

Boys With Coats

When I was ten, outside the Govan Plaza,
My first day on the Glasgow Underground,
I gave a boy with no coat in the sleet and rain
My pocket-money and my model aeroplane.
He said he was going to Greenock, the place
For which our bus was named, 'via Inchinnan'
Where we lived in village comfort near
An aerodrome—HMS *Sanderling*,
Its concrete fields of war named for a bird
I'd never seen. 'My father's in Greenock,'
He said; but the conductress wouldn't let him on.
Faces through streaming windows stared contempt
To see him set off in the wet to Linthouse,
Where they all guessed he lived—the tenements
That frightened me because they were so dark.

I who had sat in Monty's staff car at the Motor Show,
Having been born on the night of Alamein
In the war that serving justice served injustice—
That boys with coats might give to those without,
Effacing rights of ownership with gifts—
Felt radical that my lost Hurricane
Solved nothing in the sleet and rain.

Sailing with the Fleet

Delivering potatoes on the sea
Seemed hardly naval. The skeleton crews
On parked destroyers waiting to be scrapped
Smoked by their mothballed guns. Our MFV
Shambled through the gusts toward the clapped
Out flagship with their grub, our galley brews
Hot in our hands, life-jacketed and gloved
Cadets in blue December, glabrous boys
Among hulk-veterans of the convoys,
She-ships their sailors probably had loved.

Two rusting *K.G. Five*-class battleships
Were tended by our spuds, twins of the two
The Japanese torpedoed off Malaya,
Our Jimmy said. Our unheroic trips,
Bill Haley on our wind-up record player,
Were less magnificent. One thousand blue
South China Sea deaths, and many sunk tons—
Dead relatives of these, whose listless ratings
Watched workmen cut away the awful guns.
Such rust-reminders. Such steel. Such waitings.

Clydesiders

Men in boiler-suits zip twice, Clyde-built.
Thirsts, you come to this, a gush against the Shanks,
Fag-ends in the urinal, Navy Cut
Of yellow leaf, little boats of Capstan
Along the trough, blue-bottles on a crust,
And down the drain, grey ash of smokers' silt.

My poems should be Clyde-built, crude and sure,
With images of those dole-deployed
To honour the indomitable Reds,
Clydesiders of slant steel and angled cranes;
A poetry of nuts and bolts, born, bred,
Embattled by the Clyde, tight and impure.

My footprints tread a rug of settled sawdust,
The carpentering corner of a Yard.
I made these marks, have gone back to London,
No victim of my place, but mad for it.
A shower of rain, my footprints melt and run.
They'll follow to my life. I know they must.

Caledonian Moonlight

The white moon opens over a ridge of bracken
Spilling its prodigal rays into the eyes
Of the last pair of wildcat in the county
Looking for the kittens of their sterility
In the wiry heather

And the beautiful white face of a secretary
Rises in the shut eyes of a bachelor caretaker
Whose mother is dreaming
Of handing a plate of sandwiches to the minister

There are more moons in the night
Than eyes of those who see them
Open, venereal

Going to Bed

Free as the frequent rain,
And our footprints rise from their deepest marks
Till the globe is smooth of us again.

'Mundus senescit' says my priest.
The world grows old in moonlight.
And more than that, the world was always old.

Love, who is warm?
Even at this hour, the motorbikes
Gurgle their vehemences,

All-night taxis huddle round the telephone,
Sonorous locomotives pull away from time
Into the night of may-blossom,

Night that subdues the verticals
And leaves the world flat, its floating lights
Pulsing, excited hearts of predators.

Once, to a girl, I said, 'Hell is hard.
Forget me. That's easy.' And was that bad?
But being bored is full of such surprises.

And now we fly, not mattering much,
And only then to you and I,
Pale ecstasisers in a glade of rooms

When just by looking we can see our minds
Or with our fingers turn the moon
Of this excited May, to see its other side,

The Apple-Island and our carnal truth
Hushed out of its confusion by
Physical orchards, slowed rush of waves.

I Am a Cameraman

They suffer, and I catch only the surface.
The rest is inexpressible, beyond
What can be recorded. You can't be them.
If they'd talk to you, you might guess
What pain is like though they might spit on you.

Film is just a reflection
Of the matchless despair of the century.
There have been twenty centuries since charity began.
Indignation is day-to-day stuff;
It keeps us off the streets, it keeps us watching.

Film has no words of its own.
It is a silent waste of things happening
Without us, when it is too late to help.
What of the dignity of those caught suffering?
It hurts me. I robbed them of privacy.

My young friends think Film will be all of Art.
It will be revolutionary proof.
Their films will not guess wrongly and will not lie.
They'll film what is happening behind barbed wire.
They'll always know the truth and be famous.

Politics softens everything.
Truth is known only to its victims.
All else is photographs—a documentary
The starving and the playboys perish in.
Life disguises itself with professionalism.

Life tells the biggest lies of all,
And draws wages from itself.
Truth is a landscape the saintly tribes live on,
And all the lenses of Japan and Germany
Wouldn't know how to focus on it.

Life flickers on the frame like beautiful hummingbirds.
That is the film that always comes out blank.
The painting the artist can't get shapes to fit.
The poem that shrugs off every word you try.
The music no one has ever heard.

Ars Poetica

A Story

'This poem looks as if it had been written by a typewriter on a typewriter.'—Randall Jarrell

Typewriters go clip-clop,
Stupid horses making their own ways to the glue factory.

They confess small poems
Dark as prunes, but not so juicy.

One summer night when I was walking down
The street where young men rent garrets,

A voice shouted at me to come on up.
Perhaps one of my friends had moved in there.

The open window was beautiful,
Electric light made the top of the tree night-green

And the house was very old and serious,
Brooding on the long time it had been there.

I went up the stairs to the top,
Past the decorators' ladders, a pram,

Cat boxes out to air, and chained bicycles.
I went straight to the sound of typewriting.

There was nobody there.
The machine was going by itself;

Keys went down without the help of fingers,
Rising back to an unwritten smoothness

Like footprints on soft wet sand.
Heaps of poems were everywhere.

I read a few of the poems—Nothing like mine,
I thought, and looked out the window.

There were a few small moths asleep
On the curtains, and from a nail

Hammered into the wall
Plaster was dripping like white blood.

Someone's just moved in, I thought.
I shouted for them. My answer

Was the typewriter's manic plod.
There was a bottle of milk on the table.

It had gone off. A cup of tea was cold.
I put my finger in it, through the milk-film.

It clung like a nylon stocking, that colour.
There was a mouldy thin French loaf.

It was like a dildo—
One of these days, I must stop saying what things look like.

And on a stained day-bed were odds and ends
Of girlish underwear. Then I noticed

Cigarettes in an ashtray, a coffee-tin's lid,
Beside the nine assorted lipsticks.

'Move in,' urged a still small what's-it.
'This must be where the Muses hang out,

The squalid hutch of the iambic line.
At last, your chance to score big. The Nine!'

Then the door closed, and the window closed.
I couldn't get out. The typewriter kept going.

I could hear a party in the flat below.
Who were they favouring, for God's sake?

I put my ear to the floor. No, it couldn't be,
Not Adrian Henri and all that crowd!

The typewriter just kept going, on and on.
I looked at the paper. It said,

'We are the Typewriter Muses, we were bred
By W. C. Williams on Patience Strong.

We hate black ink, and those who've read
The products of that Other Nine,

Old hags inspiring crafty crap
As regular as the Renaissance.

Now drink the tea and eat the bread,
Then piss off and don't come back.'

Dear Muse, small feet and inky hands,
I ran straight home and had a bath.

I cuddled all my dictionaries,
And vowed to write forever in black ink,

Preferring better what I understand,
My life with girls' lives, and wearing black.

A Lost Woman

These lines were found inside a volume of Thomas Hardy's poems. They were written by an old man, during the last days of his life, in a summer of the 1920s.

Fog-fauntleroys at dawn, and deft
Hallucinations that a governess
In Henry James would know, when she was left
Alone, the children gone with their
Most absent father to a beach or fair—
The garden mists, those ghosts of happiness.

Dead life, so much proportion, so
Much growth is no preventer; you persist
Like amaranth. You are what some must know,
To whom, though fogs evaporate
Their fluid symmetries, the sun comes late
And moral parents wreck the furtive tryst.

Little deaths, over and over
And over, the girl in black, the heroine
On lustral walks, that life she must recover
From Sapphic hags of circumstance!
Am I occult? her soul and her remembrance?
For I remember she would not go in

One summer night, and walked about
The lawn, her eyes on nothing, seeing all
Inside her as a noxious web. That lout,

My father, called her name, his hand
On a decanter, window wide, a stand
Of billiard cues half-glimpsed against the wall.

Her name! Contemptible, and clear,
And he had said it, much against his will.
'Damn that woman! What's wrong with her?' See her,
She is of always, with lilies
By the lily pond, with fruit beneath the trees.
And who can tolerate such thick survival?

But I can talk to that mouth I
Cannot kiss; and her hand, my hand, must hold
Tight together, and neither of us die.
By adust walls, or the sun dial,
Let life and time be free, no cark, or trial—
Ah, her shadow moves, only I grow old,

She died before, she cannot die!
And I falter on paths grandfather cut
Through woods once nobly hunted, and the sky
Reaches for me, and the hounds bay
Far off, my sister, woman gone away
Not ever, and not yet, where night's doors shut.

The Concert

(For Peter Porter)

The last piano in the world
Is about to be played
In a room empty of all other furniture.
There are parts of the floor you cannot stand on.
These parts are called 'holes'.

The pianist has the last clean white shirt,
The last hale suit with tails.
Some people won't believe
Our sponsors found a piece of soap
For him to wash his hands.
But he has no shoes.
Alas, there are no longer any shoes.

And the room fills with people,
Apart from those parts called 'holes' in the old language.
But some stand on the ground, in the 'holes',
With their heads looking over the floorboards,
Through ragged trousers, women's legs.

Latecomers sit outside in the long grass,
Among the foxgloves, thick vines of ivy
That strangle the plains, playing with
Stale, blanched bones of the unfortunate.

The old ones of the audience
Anticipate the works of Bach,
Mozart, Scriabin, Beethoven,
Debussy, Chopin, Liszt.

They are just names to them,
Names that make them think, or hum
What was written by someone else.

And the pianist sits down,
And the people remember to clap.
Then the old pianist weeps.
For all he can remember
Is *Three Blind Mice.*

The Opportunity

Still with us, if we step out
Of our expensive rags
On legs as delicate as nerves
Into the grass the ad-men photograph—

The reliable stuff,
Where eyes we have forgotten
See us changed, the sanity
That is welcome, that smiles;

Where telephones don't ring,
The mail is life-times late;
Where nothing could be said against us
And the tunes are festive.

The Dilemma

Far-off summer lights
Unwritten or undiscovered masterpieces
Impossible windows

Could I traverse this valley tonight
You, neglected spark, might flame
A passion of present events

And if I did cross the valley tonight
Over the lumpy river, obstacle ridges
And you, light, are just electric
What would I do in the garden before that house?
It is perfection, to be without hope.

The White Poet

Homage to Jules Laforgue

I've travelled by the ice-floes
Purer than purest first white communicants.
I don't go to church . . .
I'm the High Chancellor of Insight,
Remember that . . .

I am a random harvest of cells,
Thinking, farting, married.
I could have been the perfect husband—
The whispering of her long dress over the carpet
In the next room is a magic hush-hush.

My shoes have walked cobblers' miles
On the backstreets. Rain, and spires of factories
In the rain . . . pianos in all the houses—
Agoraphobic furniture drizzle would love to warp.
The keyboard, an international gutter.

Pianos in the prim districts are playing
Tedious waltzes, the music of moderation.
And over the domes of swimming-baths
A clarinet's chalumeau tune drags from subterranean woods
Amazing possibilities of Priapus.

All Saints, Margaret Street, a wedding in a doorway
Touted by photographers, waiting for a cab . . .
Red-brick palace, streaming, baked,
Naked in its numbered days, hallowing the weddings
Of ill-dressed parties without taxis.

And the melancholy horns! Sad, undersea
Deranged tan-tivvy, dislocated fanfare!
Driven on the North Wind, ta-ra! ta-ta!
Turning the head of the groom who stands
Like a gland ripped from a throat.

Tanneries, chemical works, docks, post offices,
Brassy flourish of work, the diseased architecture—
Fog-flecked spittle solid on the soul.
Nature, stale factory of sap with the frenzied stink,
Is no one in love?

Or is *this* love?
All night, Our Lady of the Evenings
Never makes her mind up. Her leave-takings
Are the swishes of black dresses,
She loves a box of brutal adornments—

A gross Gothic of smoke and bubbling vats,
A Northern torch of furnaces
And Sunday afternoons of business districts
Evaporated of their carnal typists.
Hypochondria and slaughter!

Chattering in the streets, chattering in the shops,
Small talk of commercial companionships—
Where the corner-shop is an off-licence, the delicatessen
Is usually closed. That street is pretty.
This is what is meant by a City. That is the lesson.

And railway stations, breathless at the platform's end—
How lovely to look at, those trains we miss!
Gentlemen, lift the seat! Gone, without me!
Splendid, splendid, to leave the friend
Waiting with his watch in the specified pub.

Moon-woman, lover, I would gladly wring from you
White bodies of the populace
To save them, but you laugh,
Offering your ligature of nebulous caresses,
Pale oddities, mottoes of madness

And nothing to grab hold of. Moon, sick angel
Suspended through stages of globular striptease,
You vanish like love, the personality
Sipped through ice, the woman's lips on her Daiquiri—
Crushed, fragile pink drizzle in blankness.

God so loved the world
He puked every time he looked at it,
With a few miraculous exceptions. He's gone now.
Sundays, and parked cars of visitors, special joints
Like amputated stumps oozing in the ovens.

And it is the day of *The Moderation Waltz*—
    We will not buy the best, *one two three*
    We won't beat our breasts, *one two three*
    And we'll have no truck
    With that muck
    In foreign restaurants, *da-da dum-dum*

Paupers are swimming through their blood
To meet their other parents at the far end
Where fauntleroys picnic in stable sunshine
And father punts mother on the river
To the crystal honeymoon.

O waves of honey, Moon, perambulators, gloves!
Useless apostrophes!
The world is passionate as insomnia—
Insomnia of power stations sailing
In self-generated glows like bulky saints;

Insomnia of engines that start with a twist;
Insomnia of police forces, watching
Vulnerable depots of money;
Ships on their incessant stagger;
Insomniac clocks, hysterically

Ticking, the tick-tick-tock
And obliging semaphore
On the complaisant eye
Of the clock—punctual, early, late,
And remember you must die.

Sundays, time-locks, vaults, factories—
Over the land of Sunday, my wet love,
I stretch my hand.
What joins us is an ampersand.
It's easier for us. Should I take off my glove?

Should I cry in the streets, or sail over the rooftops—
Silver Street, Holy Trinity, the Guildhall, Whitefriargate—
Dropping leaflets?
Toddle off, my songs; go to the lutes
Of untuned strings, played by God's mutes,

And make no mark, subside with no pock
Or ripple in the sane mud. More dirt, more dirt!
In the botched fog of outcries, the political sandwiches—
The sky is high, and so am I—
Ah, they say, the same neat suit and tidy ties.

Privacies

The interior of a jewel,
Dark days in June;
Drifted personality, into
And out of true self; dark days,
Exclusive warp of individuals.

And the science known to a few,
All beauties locked up in galleries;
Eight million volumes on shelves
Low-born old women dust—
Dark days of civilisation.

Variations on the Words 'Solo' and 'Exhaust'

Fan-tailed exhaust of doves, high flappers
In the communal lower sky, rise above
Glutted rose-beds, pathetic brussels sprouts
That are regalia of lunatic peasant kings,
The green mace of garden parliaments.
Unmarried woman, doves are children
Of your dreams, flocking to their father.
Solitary gentlemen walk through the gate
Of the solo moon into the floating rooms
Of exhaustion, the tired singularity
Of flying on dirigible sofas.
Solitude is a set of clothes, a ticket
To the Opera that was never used.
It is so tiring. Look at your hands, that
Manicure that is for no one, hands
For knives and forks, a thousand small routines.
There's one sick angel finished with her wings,
Globular and single in the dreams
Of lunar partygoers, drained of earth-light,
A secret multitude of civilised
Despairs, too shy to cry out to the night's
Escort agencies, its luminous brothel
Of mad chances, and that solo computer
Hung like a white rose of sexual explosions,
And matching face with face, chance with desire.

Restraint

It lives in the body,
Interior clothing
Woven under nakedness

On constant looms. Textile
Animal, it feeds on words,
Evasions that trick

What might have been
To what was never tried.
It laughs its head off

At funerals, is safe
And satisfied, the only
Creature ever satisfied.

A long course in freedom
Hurts it. It cries out
And makes you tell lies.

Thinking, from Birds to God

When the mind insists
Birds sing meanings

When I watch the telephone
Imagining other telephones
Their inter-continental wires
Planetary relays and beams
Their dials resisting fingers
Their insides vascular

Whole days
Skies fascinate with their distances
A thousand shifting colours
Hiding God's voice
Nothing that never cries out

And it wrings me more dishevelled
Than all of all Scotch whisky could . . .

Were these late days in August
I would call them canicular
Or something meretricious, like that;
But it is January, and snows
Hover—where?—and not fall to here,
On us.
          I dare not ask God anything.
But, for snowflakes, I would ask
The Devil, for I need them. And
I have not seen snow these three years.
Once I rolled in it, built walls of it,
Threw it, watched it vanish to floods . . .

And now you come out of the washed
Bronze of whisky, the glinting glasses
And the backs of people, saying
'It is hot and sticky.' Lampshades!
Paintings! Furniture, and heads!
Outside it should be wild, and is not.
Canopy of factions, blizzard,
Federate my winter with one day
Of chilly white, with wanted snows
With freezing and with nothing hot
Where all the compass points of wind
Could churn the trees and come to blows.

The Estuarial Republic

The saltmarsh on the horizon
Signals with vertical smoke.
The ferry is brilliant
With ultimate parties,
A revelry of pistons,
Flushing lavatories, glasses
In hands and at shouting mouths.

The dark bed opens its mouth and howls.

'Here is a ticket
To the other side of the river,
It is very lazy but will get you there.
Here are some coins; here is the hat
You wear on deck, by the life-rafts.
Here are the gumboots
For the saltmarsh with the hulks,
It is stupid to get your feet wet.
Here are silver bullets and a gun
To defend yourself with,
It is every man's right to carry one there.
Here is the notepaper,
And the birthday pen. Come when you can
But first drop us a line.
You won't like all of it,
But the danger is fun,
And everyone visits, at least once.
You will get a chance to shoot someone,
For the horsemen raid us,
And *that* is fun. They are so stupid and reckless,

They love to die in battle,
It's a pity they are so handsome.
Their code is such it doesn't matter
Much if we just shoot them down.
Our stockade is ditched and barbed,
And you will love
The violence of our passions,
If not at first.'

The Disguise

A funeral procession of barges
On industrial canals—
The nineteenth century, and last,
Celebrating itself, through counties
Ditched and bricked with its epitaphs.

History is illiterate.
It is 'effects', wars, 'conditions',
Boots at dawn and the closing of doors,
Ambition at its conferences.
Most live in an aftermath of its injustices.

And they say, 'Go out smiling, let your poems
Tickle the ribs of Optimism
On an absolute prosody that ticks over
With the strength of an intricate machine,
Not this free verse you can buy at Woolworths.'

But I *am* smiling, and against you.
There is an invective of grins, winks, fingers,
Up the sleeves of galactic offspring.
Through your trash go their impertinent smiles,
Hidden by glum masks, the finest insult.

Acknowledgements

Acknowledgements and thanks are due to the editors of the following magazines and anthologies, in which some of these poems first appeared—*Antaeus*; *Encounter*; *Listener*; *London Magazine*; *Meridian*; *New Statesman*; *New Yorker*; *Phoenix*; *Poetry Book Society Bulletin*; *Poetry Nation*; *Prospice*; *The Review*; *Stand*; *Times Literary Supplement*; *Wave*; and *Yorkshire Arts Association Bulletin*.
Also, BBC Radio 3; and BBC Scotland.